from

Stressy & Messy

to

Organized & Optimized

How to Win the Never-Ending
Battle with Your Stuff

BOBBY JACKSON

Table of Contents

Introduction

Imagine walking into an upscale, home-decor store; the second you walk in, your heart rate drops and suddenly it's as if you are aware of every breath you take. You are in an ethereal dream world. You run your hands across the smooth edges of the gray and white, marble countertop admiring the clean lines of the model kitchens. You dive deeper into further wonders of the space. The arrangement of the rugs with the perfect sectional sofa and surrounding chairs is something you envision having in your own home one day. The light fixtures complement the staged living room without fault. *How do you feel in this very moment?*

For me, my mind is crystal clear. A warm surge overcomes every neuron in my body. I feel at peace with myself and with the world. This is a natural experience for most people, but why is that?

In my early twenties, I had the ability to do some deep soul-searching to find out what promoted tranquility and harmony within myself. *What truly makes me happy in the moment*? I came up with a list, which I do quite often, and then prioritized the options on that list to come up with my top three results:

1. Being present in my home where everything is organized and to my liking.

2. Having immediate access to all that I need.

3. Having the ability to be mindful and being capable of transitioning myself into a mindful state whenever I am on the verge of straying away from that path.

What I mean by *mindfulness* is not just being aware of my surroundings and having my mind clear, but by also adding a component of metacognition or of being aware of how I think, and how my mind personally operates. I know how I think, and I can pre-emptively determine how I am going to think and react to situations before they even arise. I am in constant control of my emotions.

This combination of almost permanent mindful and metacognitive skills is a blessing in my eyes. If you have the ability to become aware of how you think, how you learn and study to best retain knowledge, and specifically, how to make yourself happy, I recommend you take full advantage of this.

One thing I discovered through this process is that I am a visual learner like many people. When I view diagrams, models, color-coded items, tutorials, etc., I am easily able to learn the information presented to me. Studies show that 65% of people are also visual learners. It's no wonder that people become impatient, vexed, and ultimately unhappy with themselves for lacking the ability to gain new knowledge and skills because of this learning style.

I have made leaps and bounds with my career in the education field and have been very successful. I have now worked in the field of education for over five years and for most of those years I was a successful teacher. I am a college adjunct professor of Forensic Sciences, Anatomy & Physiology, and STEM Education. I have also been a high school Biology and Biomedical Science teacher for over five years and now help oversee the K-12 science departments in my school district as a Science Teacher Specialist at the Board of Education. I was even a National and State recognized science teacher receiving multiple awards and accolades from state and national science teaching organizations. All of this, being achieved at 29 years old. I don't say any of this to brag. I'm sharing my accomplishments because I can honestly say I attribute my career success to my organization, mindfulness, and metacognitive skills.

By knowing I am a visual learner, I have adjusted my life and professional work to accommodate this. Moreover, I have discovered in the teaching field, that the majority of my students I taught were also visual learners.

Why is this important?

By knowing you are a visual learner, you know that seeing images, diagrams, graphs, charts, etc., can help you learn new information better and will help you recall that information. However, I think in addition to being a visual learner, you need to learn how to be a "visual strategist." What this means is that you have to convert information that may not be shown as "visually appealing" into a format that will help you learn best.

Visual Strategist Example:

When I was an undergraduate and graduate student in college, I had to memorize many concepts in Biology. I would have a quiz the next class period in which I would need to study the 200 slides of PowerPoints the professor went over, a majority of them being words without images. For me, it was rather difficult to just read each slide of notes and try to remember everything.

Having metacognitive skills, I was able to realize early on the best study habits for myself. In order to be successful, I decided to print out the PowerPoints with six slides per page. I numbered each page and I made a unique, colored shape for each slide. For instance, slide 42 has a green triangle in the upper right-hand corner of it. Slide 133 would have a blue heart in the bottom left corner. Slide 193 depicts a purple star in the bottom left corner.

See the picture? When I went to take my assessments, I was able to have my brain navigate to the exact slide the question and/or answer was mentioned on. The products of photosynthesis were mentioned on page nine on the bottom right slide that had an orange circle. Now that my brain had mentally located where that slide was, I can distinctly recall the verbiage on that slide: glucose and oxygen. Of course, the content became much more advanced in Immunology, Anatomy & Physiology, Cell Biology, etc., and I still was able to excel in these rigorous courses. Thankfully, I later realized that this contributed to the need for organization in my life.

So I'm sure as a reader, you are wondering why I am rambling on about education, learning capabilities, and mindfulness when this is supposed to be a book about organizational strategies? But before I get to this answer, let's go back to my list of top three things that make me at peace, thereby making me happy:

1. Being present in my home that is organized and to my liking.

2. Having immediate access to everything I need.

3. Having the ability to be mindful and being capable of transitioning myself into a mindful state whenever I was on the verge of straying away from that path.

Having my home immaculate and customized to my own liking with complete tidiness, and plenty of space to walk, with decorations of my own choosing, pleases me. Being present in a space where my carpets always seem fresh and vacuumed, my clothing in my closet and

vi · BOBBY JACKSON

drawers are fully organized without being cluttered, my kitchen countertops are spotless…I could go on for hours complimenting my house. What I'm trying to say is, I am fully satisfied with my home and therefore, when I am home, I am at peace. I have a clear mind, a clear soul, and am clearly happy with myself and my accomplishments for having established this home.

I want this for you too because I know how much peace and serenity you will have in your life when it is organized, orderly, and functional.

It's funny to me now, but some people refer to me as the "Connoisseur" of Organization. In college, I had color-coded binders for each course, with color-coded tabs, study guides, sheets, etc. I transferred this organizing obsession into my home, my closet, my kitchen, my bathroom, my living room, and every space I had. When I thought I had reached my peak of being fully organized, with every tangible aspect of my life being as pristine as I envisioned, I still felt an uneasiness. A presence of inadequacy still remained.

How is this even possible?

It was then that I performed deeper soul searching and delved into my second priority: I needed to have immediate access to everything. Although I was beyond pleased with my home and the organization of everything within it, I still felt as though something was missing. If I had a cocktail party I had planned to go to, I knew of the exact location of the shirt, pants, and shoes I planned on wearing for such an event. If I wanted to look up a quote

I distinctly remember from a book I had read, I knew the exact location of that book within my home.

However, if someone asked me for a specific email someone had sent me three months ago, or a file that was sent to me eight months ago, I would be extremely nervous and unsure of myself in being able to retrieve those files and pieces of evidence. It was then that I had an epiphany.

I WAS AN EXPERT IN PHYSICAL ORGANIZATION BUT AN AMATEUR IN ELECTRONIC/DIGITAL ORGANIZATION.

It was a new world I never imagined or even considered to dive into. This is a problem, not just for me, but for so many other people as well. As a result, I decided to put my knowledge to use and I have an entire section in this book dedicated to electronic and digital organization.

Because of my organizing skills, I became the go to person for my friends, family, colleagues, and even acquaintances to help them organize their homes, clothes, drawers, miscellaneous items, etc. What's interesting is that I have never heard of anyone asking for help with "electronic organization."

I decided to do a little research online about electronic organization and I found nothing. It was then that I felt the need to take it upon myself to be the pioneer of this new adventure in digital organizing. Years later, I became an expert in the new field of what I dub "electronic and digital organization." I have helped many adults and students in this "hidden area," which is why I am choosing to write this book on not just how you can organize your home and your physical space, but also your electronic world as well.

Digital organization can include things like emails, downloads, website-addresses, electronic files and folders, apps on your cell phone, photographs and even music playlists. There are so many things we do on a daily basis for both work and pleasure that it's evidently critical that we become electronically organized.

When I finally was able to consider myself an expert in physical, mental, and now electronic organization, it was then that I was fully at peace with myself. I can say that I have experienced a high level of contentment ever since.

I hope the strategies I share in this book will help you on your organization journey. I know without a doubt that being organized will bring you more peace, serenity, and will also save you time. This book contains my personal organization strategies that you can immediately apply to your everyday life that will ultimately lead you to being content as well.

FAST ACTION IMPLEMENTATION

1. Search online for a Visual, Auditory, and Kinesthetic Learning Quiz/Survey to see what type of learner you are. *Education Planner* is a great resource to

use to discover your learning preference. Just complete 20 questions to find out:

http://www.educationplanner.org/students/self-assessments/learning-styles-quiz.shtml

2. Decide if your main need for organization falls under electronic or physical organization. Focus on one area at a time. Part one of this book is for digital organization and part two of this book is for physical organization.

Why I Wrote This Book

Sometimes we are blind to our own strengths. My organizing skills were something I actually took for granted and didn't think much about. As I mentioned, I am in the education field and it was my students who pointed this out to me first. Whether it was through verbal conversations, course evaluations, etc., it was repetitively mentioned over and over again.

It was then I decided to take notes on my organizational techniques and strategies. In my science classroom, I took time to assist students with ways they could increase their organization to make them college and career ready. Many of my students learned these concepts and took them in stride.

I was not only organized in a professional setting, but in a domestic one as well. Since my college dormitory, to my apartment, then a 1,600 square foot home to now a 7,100 square foot single family home, my homes have always been pristine. No matter what size, I have found ways to make my home permanently organized using the methods I outline in this book. These methods will accommodate all varieties of living spaces.

I have read several books on organization but have come to find that most of them involve just physical organization techniques. Although physical organization is pivotal, I have found that digital organization is just as important these days and is something that should not be overlooked. The information out there on books and guides on electronic organizing is extremely limited.

This has led me to write this book on both physical and digital organization. However, I do not just want to provide factual and straight-forward information on strategies that you can implement in your own home. I think it is very important to understand the "why" behind organization.

- *Why are people not always organized?*
- *Why do people attempt to be organized and then relapse back into physical and electronic anarchy and clutter?*
- *Why do individuals fall back into these bad habits knowing it causes them so much stress?*
- *Why be stressed out and messy, when people can be organized, and then become the best versions of themselves, thereby optimizing their lives?*

This book therefore takes a psychological approach in addition to a strategical approach that digs deep into the mind. Organization also serves as a mindful technique. It allows people to become aware of their surroundings. It makes them stress-free, and ultimately can make them happy. I want to share this version of organization with the world. I want you to realize that organization can be your *yoga*, if you alter your mindset to allow it to. Let me be the one to help you become organized and be the most optimized version of yourself. Let's get organized together and have fun while doing so. Let's take a journey to organization nirvana!

The 3 Biggest Mistakes People Make When It Comes to Organizing

My goal is for you to be uber-successful on this journey to getting organized and optimized. Your success is my success! Unfortunately, not everyone is born with this organization gene; I've discovered that the majority of people have to work hard at it. So don't feel bad. It is definitely a learned skill and as you use this new skill, you will become better and better at it. Just know that even if being organized wasn't something you were taught when you were younger or in school, you still stand a chance.

In working with and observing others, I've noticed three common mistakes that people make on their journey to getting more organized and I want to save you from these mistakes before we begin.

Mistake #1: People Organize without Decluttering first

Organizing can be fun and exciting especially when it involves shopping at places like "The Container Store" for fancy bins, baskets, containers, and even complete organizing systems. The intention is good. We do need systems and organizing bins and containers to put our stuff in because it helps us to find things and assists with sorting items out. However, before we get to this part, we want to declutter FIRST.

When you organize first without decluttering here is what happens…

You are ready to start organizing your closet, full of books, clothing and shoes that are years old. You go to your favorite retail store and are excited because you have an idea of how you want to reorganize this space. You decide to buy various storage bins with bright, vibrant colors. Your goal is to have a color-coded system to attack this mess in your closet. When you get home, you empty out your closet and reorganize the same stuff by sorting it out and placing that "old" stuff into your "new" colorful boxes and bins.

You now have dozens of stacked boxes in your closet that look pretty but take up way too much space. Your belongings are hard to get to and now you are just storing things you haven't used in months or years and probably aren't ever going to use again.

I don't want you to waste money on organizing materials that you don't need. Whether you are organizing your computer files or your bedroom closet, you MUST declutter and get rid of things you are not using. If you haven't used an item in 12 months, I would highly recommend getting rid of it.

It's easy to think that organizing and decluttering mean the same thing, but they don't. Decluttering is removing things from your home (or devices) that you are not using and will probably never need or use. Organizing is creating a system and a space for the things you do use and need. In this book, I also include methods on how to declutter throughout many chapters.

Mistake #2: When you are repeatedly organizing the same space over and over.

It's frustrating to have to continuously keep organizing the same space. For example, if your office or bedroom gets disorganized after a few weeks or even if you found yourself needing to reorganize that space after just recently fully cleaning it up a few months ago, that's a red flag that you have too much stuff in that space. One thing that can help is to have a friend who is good at organization or decluttering come over and help you get rid of things.

A friend of mine was very sentimental about all of her belongings and had a hard time getting rid of stuff. One area that was constantly a disaster was her garage. So, she asked me to help her clean out the garage and I happily agreed. Lucky for her, I am very fast at making decisions.

My method was to give her 30 seconds to make a decision and if she didn't make a decision, that item went in the trash. She had 30 seconds to decide: *trash, keep, or donate*. When she said "keep" I would then ask her when the last time she used that item was and to give me a reason why she should keep it. This made her logical brain kick in, instead of her emotions, and before you know it, the garage was decluttered and subsequently organized.

Mistake #3: Dreading Organizing Your Space.

For many people, the process of organizing and decluttering is seen as a chore and they want to avoid it like the plague. However, consider the amount of time you spend and waste looking for stuff you can't find. Also, if you have a great deal of disorganization in your home, then you probably aren't feeling very peaceful, serene or calm. Studies have shown that clutter and messes cause anxiety and stress on a physiological level.

So, let's make a mind-shift and instead of viewing organizing and decluttering as a chore, let's look at it as a way to add more peace and serenity to your life as well as "time." Wouldn't you love walking into a beautifully organized home where you are able to find everything you need and when you need it, instead of feeling frustrated and angry because you don't know where your stuff is?

You need to have fun organizing your stuff and remove all that unnecessary anxiety and stress from your life! My favorite way to relax before I begin organizing or decluttering is to have a glass of wine. Wine is a great way to relax and get in the mode of decluttering and organizing.

Part I – Digital Organization

Chapter 1:
The Mindset of Highly Organized People

Before you venture out to start your organization journey, you need to make sure you are in the right mindset to do so. If you are not in the right mindset, you face a greater risk of relapsing into what I call "physical and electronic anarchy." The mentality it takes to start making a drastic, new change to your current lifestyle requires deep focus and willpower.

To make you understand what it takes, let's compare the process of organization to the process of going on a new healthy diet or beginning a new fitness workout. People who have a lack of motivation and cannot maintain a strong willpower will often relapse and not be able to sustain the healthy diet and lifestyle they want to achieve. One cheat day a week may eventually turn into permanent cheat days if your mental awareness is not on point.

Sticking to an organizational routine works in the same way. You may think "Oh, that piece of mail can sit on the side table for now. When I move into the next room, I'll take it with me." The human mind becomes so consumed with more prioritized thoughts or thoughts about things you are more interested in at the time, that the piece of mail takes a back seat in the brain. It will most likely become ignored and then the process repeats itself until you wind up with "physical anarchy" in your home.

I want you to take a moment to close your eyes. Visualize your ideal perfect home. Imagine a place you can return to after a long stressful day at work. When you come in through the front door, the ambiance is so appealing. There is no piece of paper or mail or clothing or coat or anything out of place. Your home is beautifully decorated and whether you decide to have a glass of wine and read a book, go into the office or sit on the sofa and work on your laptop, or even prep for dinner, you are able to take a deep breath and smile knowing everything is in order as it should be. You are relaxed, at ease, and overall…you are happy. You deserve that glass of wine! Sip up!

If you do not think you are in the right mindset to be able to perform such a new, tedious task in organizing everything around you, fear not. There are ways to put yourself into the mindset to be able to be organized and to maintain that organization. The best way to do this is through metacognition. I mentioned this earlier and I want to explain it a little bit more here.

Metacognition is having the ability to understand your own thought processes and how your mind works. It sounds like something unattainable. You either have it or you don't have it, right? Wrong. Metacognition is a skill anyone can obtain. Just like any skill, it just takes a little bit of practice. The best way to understand your own mind is through the process of constant *reflection*.

As a former teacher, one of the most beneficial instructional strategies that has helped my students in the long run with developing higher-order and critical thinking skills is reflection. No one should ever underestimate the power of reflection. In my experience, I know of many teachers who do not utilize this opportunity for their students, although they are not completely at fault. Many teachers are caught up in a long curriculum, where they need as much time as possible to get through all of the required standards to make their students successful in the classroom. They realize there is not enough time in their class periods for reflection. This, however, is not true. There are so many ways where opportunities for reflection can occur in the classroom. It just takes a little bit of creative thinking and reorganizing on the teacher's end to make it happen.

In my classroom, reflection took place in the form of a journal, an exit ticket, a creative-writing prompt, or even giving students the opportunity to complete revisions on work that I provided them critical feedback on. Reflections should always be presented in a way where students have newfound knowledge and they explain that newfound knowledge while also describing what their background was on the topic before they learned it. For instance, a typical reflection response in one of my Anatomy & Physiology classes might be: "Before this unit, I thought cholesterol was bad for your body. I have now learned that there are two types of cholesterol – LDL, being the 'bad' cholesterol and HDL, being the 'good' cholesterol."

So why is reflection so important for students and all individuals? The more reflection that takes place, the more the individual realizes its importance, especially during learning experiences. People realize their previous misconceptions or initial assumptions and they are then able to realize how this may have impacted their learning. Now, this individual is thinking about their learning process, thereby being metacognitive.

Metacognition is fundamentally a form of reflection. The more reflective thinking that is practiced, the more developed your metacognitive skills are becoming. Once you develop metacognition, you are able to come to a realization based on your previous organization skills. You will begin to wonder and ask questions like *What kept me from being organized? Why have I not been organized all along? What has prevented me from having all of my clothing in the closet in a neat array on hangers? Why am I now seeking to organize all of my electronic files?"* It's questions like these, that open the doors to the answers. So asking these types of questions, will help you through this process. Once you are confident in your answers, then it is time to proceed with my organizational strategies.

FAST ACTION IMPLEMENTATION

1. Develop a journal log or diary describing your experience with organization and reflect on it.

2. Write down the answers to the following questions:

- What kept me from being organized?
- Why have I not been organized all along?
- What areas around my house (physically) or electronically do I want to focus on first?
- Why am I now seeking to organize physical and electronic spaces?

Chapter 2:
The True Agenda
Behind Organization

I want to remind you of the "end goal in mind." Yes, we may want to be organized in order to impress our friends, or so that we are easily able to find anything and know where every item in our home is as a result of designating a permanent location for them. However, these are not the true end goals. These are merely objectives that support the end goal. The end goal I'm referring to is "happiness." The reason we should seek to establish organization in our lives is to put us at peace, and to allow our minds to seek serenity.

It's also imperative to look at the opposite end of that spectrum. We can also view the end goal as reducing the amount of stress that comes with "physical anarchy," which thereby would lead us to a healthy mind that is full of euphoria and prosperity.

When my life is completely organized, my mind is also completely organized, and I am my best self. I want you to repeat this out loud as you work to organize your life: "When my life is completely organized, my mind is also completely organized, and I am my best self!"

To-Do Lists

"Change the plan but never the goal," is a comment I often made to my students and is a statement I still live by today. Once you have established an attainable goal for yourself, it would be self-destructive or self-sabotaging to alter that goal. Now you may alter your navigation towards that goal or find that modifications need to be made in order for you to reach it, but NEVER change the goal.

So, the first thing I want you to do is generate a list, whether it's on a notepad, lined piece of paper, electronic document, or whatever your preference is. I want this list to be a set of "organization goals." The more specific details that are on the list, the better. It needs to be descriptive and it should address what parts of your lifestyle you want to change in order to be more organized. Here is an example:

- I want my bedroom closet to completely change so that all of my clothes are hung on hangers, color-coded, and organized by the material or

type of clothing. I also want my sock and underwear drawer to be as neat as possible.
- I have way too many photographs scattered throughout the house. I want them all in a single location so that they are not cluttering up random drawers in multiple rooms of my home.
- My email inbox is completely out of whack! I need to find a way to organize it so that I can easily find my important emails and not lose any of them.
- My kitchen cabinets are stuffed with kitchenware and appliances all over the place and I need a better way to organize them.
- The top of my office desk is full of papers, pens, etc. I want it to be completely cleaned off and looking professional.

I would recommend this goal-oriented list have no more than five bullet points. This should not be a running list of over ten bullet points, because that would become extremely overwhelming and stressful which is the opposite of how this therapeutic process should make you feel. Also, as I mentioned earlier, these goals should be attainable. Now perhaps you may feel that you do have more than five goals in mind. However, let's just take care of the top five things we want to get organized, and then once we have completed those five, we can generate a new list of five more goals and so on. If you are unsure of where to begin, I highly recommend you review the table of contents of this book and focus on topics that will help you achieve your goals.

Once you have your goals mapped out, let's put this list somewhere where it is constantly visible, like under a magnet on the refrigerator, on a bare side table somewhere in your house, or on your main electronic computer screen using the "sticky note" application. You want to be able to access this list at all times.

Now that we have made this list, it's time to focus on goal number one. We are going to do the unthinkable! Make a list for the list or rather make a plan for the plan! We need to map out how we are going to meet goal one on your list. If goal number one on your list is related to the kitchen, then move on to the "kitchen" chapter in this book to gather ideas for your list. If goal number one is organizing your cell phone, then go directly to the chapter in this book that addresses cell phones to help you make your planned list.

The most important thing about this process is that we are ONLY FOCUSED ON ONE GOAL AT A TIME. If we decide to work on too many goals at once, we are not giving our full and undivided attention to a specific goal. Organization is a baby-step process. As I previously discussed, this should not be an overwhelming feat. We need to be mindful of our goal, our plan, and to make sure that this is cleansing to our soul. If we are not enjoying ourselves then we are not in the right frame of mind to be participating in the organization process. If you do have a slight inclination of doubt when it comes to organizing, just pour yourself a glass of wine to alleviate that doubt.

In regards to making plans to achieve goals, teachers do this all of the time with their students. There is one set goal or, what we call in education, an "essential question" that students should be able to answer by the end of a unit. The essential question should come with a multiple set of objectives that students need to achieve in order to be able to fully answer the essential question.

For long-term projects, teachers actually guide students towards the end goal or final product so that students are meeting their objectives or standards along the way. There might be extra support from teachers to push students in the proper direction, which can be in the form of what we call scaffolding or tiering, but nevertheless, it is a step by step process.

Being able to "check a box" off of our planned lists means that we are holding ourselves accountable. We are both mentally and physically assessing our completion of tasks to meet our organization goals. It's a measurable procedure that allows us to pat ourselves on the back for being efficient and for a job well done.

Speaking of efficient, you may find that one of the plans on your list is not working well or maybe you realized it needs some work or modification. This is a trial and error process. Do not ever think that once you have your plans on your list to meet your organization goal that they are set in stone. They can be altered, and actually should be, to better meet your organizational needs. As I previously stated, "change the plan, but never the goal."

Having lists is one of the most important aspects of this entire operation. It serves as a measurable checklist for us to verify that we have a set target goal in mind and that we are proceeding in the right direction to meet that goal. Making a list is Organization 101. A list has its own goal, which is to make the user organized. Name one list that you have ever seen that is not meant to provide organization?

FAST ACTION IMPLEMENTATION

1. Make a list of your top five goals you have for the organization process.

2. For each of these five goals, develop a separate list explaining how you plan on accomplishing these goals (if you need help with this, visit specific sections of this book to get ideas).

Chapter 3:
Should I Use a Planner?

We all know that one person, whether it was a roommate in college, an eager and energetic colleague, or even an over-enthusiastic friend who has a color-coded planner, where they write their itinerary in twenty different colored inks or use ten different colored highlighters to map out their weekly schedules. They have the type-A personality trait where they cannot fully function unless their deadlines and to-do lists are in sequential order with the appropriate color-scheme they deemed necessary in their planners. I was one of these individuals.

However, I was not one of the annoying types who went out of their way to show you just how organized I was and felt necessary to explain my strategic color-coding to you in the hopes of receiving some sort of self-gratification. I'm sure we have all experienced the presence of that individual at least once in our lives. Your goal with scheduling and planning should not be as extravagant as this.

Schedules and planners are a bit difficult to categorize in the realm of organization. They are fairly nebulous because many people utilize them in different formats. Some people have electronic calendars in their email systems, or even on their phones. Others prefer a yearly notebook-style planner or a large calendar on their office desk. I even know of people who keep a mental calendar in their brains of activities, dates, etc., which I do not recommend. Schedules and planners can fall under mental, physical, or electronic organization. It just depends on the user. However, I think electronic schedules and planners are the best for two reasons: alarms/reminders on upcoming events and having dates and activities being easily able to be modified.

First, let's make our planned list on how we want to be organized when it comes to utilizing schedules and planners:

- I want to have a schedule that addresses my weekly or bi-weekly duties/tasks that I routinely perform at work or at home.
- I need some sort of schedule or organizer where I can keep track of important dates and appointments that could be weeks or months planned out in advance.

- I would like to have a plan in place so that I remind myself to look at my schedule everyday so that I do not miss any events or deadlines.
- I currently have an "already-made" scheduling process or used a planner in the past, but I want to make it more organized and easy to use.
- There needs to be a way that I can organize my schedule and planner that meets my specific needs for my job, education, or some form of work life.

Now that we have our planned list in place to meet our goal of having an organized schedule or planner, we can start the organization process. The first thing we need to consider is what type of schedule we want to establish. That will determine the best way to go about and maintain that schedule.

One type is a routine schedule. A routine schedule is made to show you hourly activities over the course of the week that typically remain constant. For instance, a college student might want to develop a routine schedule so they are able to block off times for their classes so that they know at what points of the day are free or available to them. A businessman may have meetings with certain employees and subordinates once a week with a set time, like 2:00pm every Tuesday. This routine or block schedule prevents them from overbooking any other meetings, appointments, or events during this time.

How should one go about making a block schedule? I highly recommend doing so electronically in a document or spreadsheet where you can access multiple tables. Below is an example of a block schedule I used in every semester during my college years.

	Monday	Tuesday	Wednesday	Thursday	Friday
9:00am	BIO 310 Lecture	CHEM 327 Lecture	BIO 310 Lecture	CHEM 327 Lecture	BIO 310 Lecture
9:30am					
10:00am					
10:30am					
11:00am	BIO 310 Lab	CHEM 327 Lab	SI Session	Work Academic Link Desk	SI Session
11:30am					
12:00pm					Work Academic Link Desk
12:30pm					
1:00pm			PHIL 360 Lecture		
1:30pm					
2:00pm					
2:30pm		BIO 330 Lecture		BIO 330 Lecture	
3:00pm	CHEM 340 Lecture		CHEM 340 Lecture		
3:30pm					
4:00pm					

It's very simple to print out a schedule like this and post it in multiple locations where you have access to it. I pinned it to my bulletin board in my dorm and put it in the front cover sleeve in most of my binders I used. As long as it's in a place where you will always have access to it, this will suffice.

When making a long-term calendar schedule, I always use my cell phone calendar. One thing that a cell phone calendar does that a written calendar does not do is send you reminders of upcoming events. Hand-written calendars are unable to do this.

Let me give you a scenario many of us have experienced in our lifetime. I am not the greatest at remembering the birthdays of some of my extended family members and friends. In the past, when technology was limited, I would jot down all of my friends' and family members' birthdays on a physical calendar. There are times when I would forget to look at that calendar on a daily occasion and I hate to admit it, but I was forced to wish some of my friends and family members a happy belated birthday as a result. How embarrassing! However, now that all birthdates are entered into my phone calendar, I get a vibration and notification every morning of a birth date, reminding me to call that individual to wish them a happy birthday.

Electronic calendars and schedules are also more useful because they can easily be modified unlike the typical notebook-style planner. Suppose you decide to make a doctor's appointment three weeks from now. In your notebook-style planner, you would most likely fill out the date and time in your calendar in colored ink. However, you later realize the appointment interferes with a pre-planned event you forgot to record. Now you are forced to scratch out the doctor's appointment in your planner and it looks like an absolute hot mess! If an electronic phone calendar were used instead, you could simply delete the doctor's appointment, reschedule it, and even add the pre-planned event to replace it. Everything still remains organized and all is right in the world! Take that glass of pinot noir and sip up! Below is a screenshot from my phone calendar as a visual model:

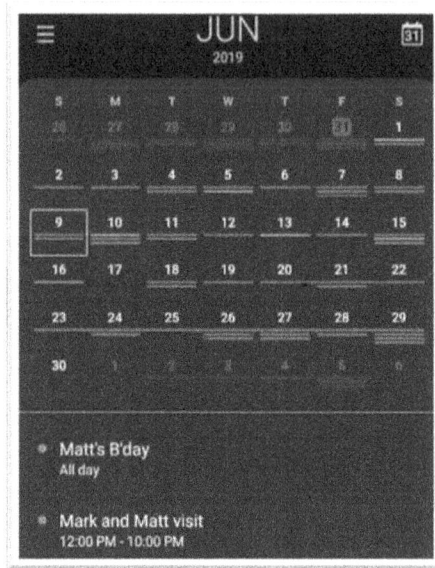

All you do is simply click on a date and add the event and time. Each event pops up as a single colored line. Now if your schedule is typically very jam packed, I highly recommend color-coding events by category. Maybe you decide to make all birthdays red, social events in blue, and work-related activities in green. There are many options to consider, but as long as you organize your electronic phone calendar in a way that meets your needs, it should be efficient enough.

The big take away is "DO AWAY WITH NOTEBOOK-STYLE PLANNERS AND UTILIZE ELECTRONIC SCHEDULES AND CALENDARS." Take advantage of new technology that makes your life more efficient and that offers an easy means of organization. Remember that notebooks are permanent and cannot be altered. Once that ink meets the paper, all is said and done. If you need to make a modification, it will wind up being a scratched out mess that you are stuck with. That is not very organized at all.

Whenever you make any decision about buying or using something for organization, you should always consider the outcome of that usage. For instance, I for one will never allow glitter into my home. Although glitter might be festive and lively for holidays, birthdays, etc., I know that the joy glitter may bring at that time is short-term and very fleeting. In the end, I will wind up with specs of glitter all in my carpets and on the floor that will take multiple clean-up attempts to remove fully. In this case, the risk outweighs the reward. Always mentally weigh your risks and rewards when it comes to organization before just making a rash decision.

FAST ACTION IMPLEMENTATION

1. Go into your cell phone and add all of your family members' and friends' birthdates with "reminders on them."

2. Create a block schedule (modeled after the one I provided) to show your hourly schedule during the work week.

Chapter 4:
Desktop Disorganization

If you cannot fully see the background image on your computer or laptop, then you need to find a better means of organization. Desktop icons and folders should take up no more than a quarter of the screen. If you are having difficulty meeting this recommended standard, then this chapter will help you fix that.

Icons that automatically arise on your computer from the get go are fine to keep. This includes your "recycle bin," "my computer/this PC," etc. Major applications that are specific to your job or work are also acceptable to leave on your desktop as well as a few folders.

When I assist people with this in person, a response I traditionally get is "well, what about my internet browsers and software icons like Microsoft Word, Excel, PowerPoint, etc., that I use on a daily basis?" To this, I say that you should permanently pin internet browsers and

Microsoft applications to your bottom task bar. This can be accomplished just by simply dragging the icons from the desktop to the bottom bar of your computer. You also want to avoid cluttering your bottom task bar, so I recommend only pinning up to seven icons to the bottom task bar: two internet browsers, four of your most top used Microsoft Office applications, and the folder that will lead to all possible files on your computer.

So what if you have tons of files on your desktop and it's difficult to determine which qualifies as a desktop icon and should remain?

Make Folders

Figure out commonalities between certain files and make a folder that multiple documents, spreadsheets, PDFs, files, etc., can go into. One folder might be titled "Work Files." Another could be labeled as "Games." If you have a lot of family photos, you can create a folder titled "Family Photos 2019" or whatever year it is if you want to separate the photos by year.

Keep consolidating so that not only is your desktop screen now only a quarter full, but so that your folders make logical sense and you can easily find and access the files within them.

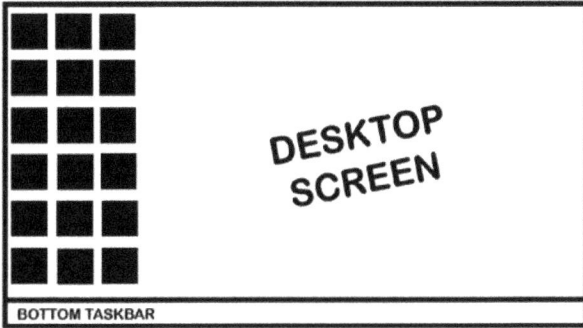

Why should you only fill up a quarter of your screen and no more? As I mentioned before, our goal for any type of organization is to be sustainable and for the user to not relapse. If your desktop screen is half-way full, you can easily wind up adding a few files to the desktop and lose the electronic organization method you had worked so hard to develop and maintain.

Another tip that I recommend for desktops is to use the "sticky note" feature. Sticky notes are literally electronic post-it notes. It is a great strategy to use in order to keep daily reminders or to make lists of tasks that you need to complete for work or errands you need to fulfill throughout the week. I use the sticky-notes feature on a daily basis. Let's not forget to mention that it is a powerful tool in organization! Now, you don't need to leave colorful post-it notes in all corners of your house as reminders. Just use the electronic version to consolidate. It will remain permanently on your desktop screen every time you open it. So you can't miss it! Lift that wine glass to your lips! Sip up!

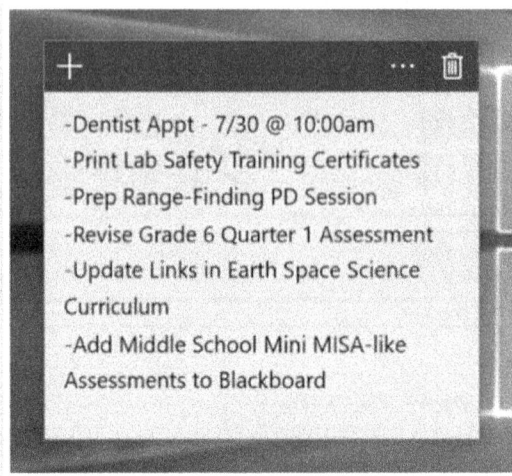

Having a clean, uncluttered desktop will put your mind at ease. Having your files organized into categorized folders will allow you to access them more easily. I have taught and recommended this technique to many students and adults. I have received nothing but positive feedback and have even had past students comment on how they distinctly remember this lesson I taught them and to this day, they still follow it.

FAST ACTION IMPLEMENTATION

1. Organize your desktop icons from left to right and combine folders to save space. Make sure you only have 25% of your desktop filled.

2. Add two internet browsers and Microsoft Office Applications to the bottom of your taskbar.

Chapter 5:
Email Hell

Imagine this…

You are at work and you are attempting to log in to an account of yours and forgot the password. The email containing your original password was sent to you months ago. You navigate through what seems an endless list of emails only to be unable to find it. This is an experience most of us have had at one point or another. This experience has happened to me as well, and it was the scenario that sparked my interest to pursue knowledge about electronic organization, a world I had never tapped into before.

First, make sure you have at least two different email accounts. One should be specifically used for work or professional purposes. The other email account will serve as the less formal of the two and should be used for more social-related emails like communication between friends, coupons from retail stores and clothing vendors, etc.

Within your email server, you should have about five folders so that not all of your emails are completely overflowing your inbox. So what exactly should the titles of these five folders be? That all depends on you. Here is the task you need to complete in order to figure out the folders to have in your email. Go through your most fifty recent emails that are present in your inbox. Grab a separate sheet of paper and organize those fifty emails into five categories. Whatever five categories you dub when you are separating these emails, those will be the five folder titles for that email account. Here is how one of my former professional email accounts was organized as an example.

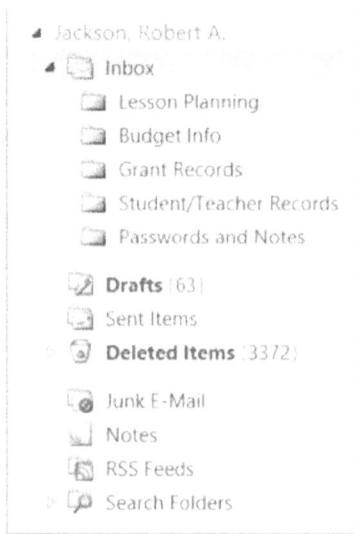

When I went back through my work-related emails, I took a step further in the organization process and actually searched through my last one-hundred emails and categorized them. As it turned out, I wound up with seven folders and there was no way I could further consolidate the emails into only five folders that made sense, or so I initially had thought. My seven folders were titled: Lesson Planning, Budget Info, Grant Records, Student Records, Teacher Records, Password, and Notes.

I then realized that I can combine some of these folders. Student Records and Teacher Records could go in the same folder with a combined title: Student/Teacher Records. The next easiest set of folders to blend that made the most sense to me was Passwords and Notes, which merged to create a single folder known as Passwords and Notes.

TRY TO KEEP YOUR EMAIL INBOX FOLDERS TO A MAXIMUM OF FIVE.

The reason I say this is because having more than five folders will lead to too many folders where it may be difficult to navigate to recover a specific email from. You do not want to have too few of folders because then those folders will end up being as full and disorganized as your original inbox, and it will be difficult to search and find important emails.

These same guidelines should also apply to your social email account. However, the folders in your inbox for this account should be even easier to organize. Using my recommended rules, you should again revisit your last fifty emails and categorize them into five folders. For most people, their inbox folders will look fairly similar, since most of us use our social email accounts for the same things. The five folders I have for my account are Social Media, Coupons and Discounts, Friends and Family, Professional/Job, and Home-Related.

For Social Media, these include any notifications or messages synced to social media accounts like Facebook, Twitter, Instagram, etc. The Coupons and Discounts folder is self-explanatory. Any emails from retail and clothing vendors that share coupons, weekend sales, or even special deals should be moved here. Any email exchanges between friends and family or emails that are relevant to any of your friends and family should get sent into the Friends and Family folder.

My last two folders require a bit of an explanation as it may not be so obvious of the type of emails that should be transferred into these folders. I'm sure you're asking, "why would you need a Professional/Job folder when you have a separate professional/work email account that should have all of your work-related files and emails?" While this is a valid question, there comes a time when many people may be searching for other job opportunities or even have multiple jobs or part-time jobs. I believe it is highly unprofessional to use your work email for searching for other jobs outside of your current employer or for other part-time jobs, so utilizing your social email account is the more appropriate solution. Also, although I work for my county school system, I also teach part-time at colleges and universities and am associated with other educational affiliations. So anytime someone needs to contact me in regards to those colleges and universities, I provide them with my personal/social email address to best reach me at. Any email that pertains to your home qualifies for the Home-Related folder. When you send emails to companies for plumbing, furniture, backyard or lawn maintenance, or are in the process of getting estimates and quotes from these associations, all of these emails get placed in the Home-Related folder.

Now as I mentioned previously, these are my five specific folders for my social or personal email account. However, I have found that others have actually used most of the same folders as well but might change one or two around to best meet their needs. Because I live in a single-family home with a backyard and front yard, I definitely need a Home-Related folder. However, some people I know live in an apartment or in a condo and therefore it is unnecessary for them to have this folder when they do not receive many emails related to their home.

There is no absolute right or wrong way to do this. As long as your organized folders meet your specific needs to your lifestyle, then your email account should now be completely organized and it will be less stressful now that you have a "process" for maintaining and handling emails. You should easily be able to access emails that were once difficult for you to search for and find. Now take that sigh of relief after you take a drink of that cabernet. Sip up!

FAST ACTION IMPLEMENTATION

1. Create two email accounts: a professional/work email and a social email account.

2. Look over your last 50 emails and categorize them. Create five folders to drag these emails into to organize your inbox.

Chapter 6:
How to Make Your
Cell Phone Smarter

I recall the days where cell phones had very limited features compared to the smart phones we see today. According to AppAnnie, the average smartphone user in the United States has about 95 applications on their phone. The most surprising statistic about this data is that about only 35 of these 95 applications are actually being used by the individual.

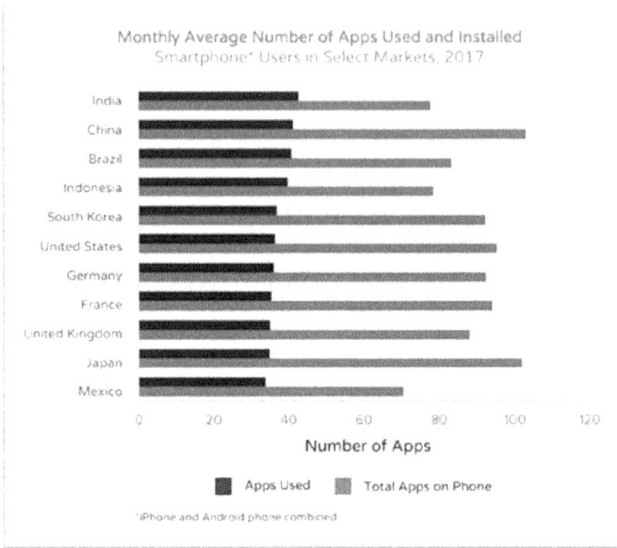

Monthly Average Number of Apps Used and Installed
Smartphone* Users in Select Markets, 2017

I found this to be true about myself as well. I had so
many apps on my phone and yet I rarely used half of
them. I still find myself adding applications and as I'm
going through the electronic organization process, I wind
up uninstalling many of them. This is a normal practice
among most people. So here is my first tip regarding apps
on phones.

Go through all of the applications in your phone once
every month or two. **IF YOU HAVE NOT USED AN APP
MORE THAN ONCE IN THE PAST TWO MONTHS,
YOU SHOULD UNINSTALL IT.** Although you may think
you will use the app in the near future, do not fall down
this dark rabbit hole and relapse. Stick to this rule or you
will end up as part of the statistic mentioned earlier.

An alternative to this strategy would be to download an application that has the ability to keep track of the amount of times you have used an application and how frequently you have used it. One of these applications that monitors all of your application usage is called "App Usage – Manage/Track Usage." There are so many other applications on the market that also perform this same function.

Now that your cell phones have only the most useful apps installed, we need to organize them. If you view each application individually, it's usually in alphabetical order. However, this is not the best way to maintain them in your phone. Plus, it may require a few scrolls through the screen just to find the app you want to use. For this reason, all applications should be on your home-screen organized into folders. Below is my home-screen on my phone.

The most commonly used phone features should be at the bottom of your home-screen. These include, text messaging, phone calls, emails, and an internet browser. I actually once had my main music application present in a folder, but because I use it multiple times a day, I felt the need to put it on my home-screen as a main icon and not restrict it to a folder. Some examples of folders you may want to include on your phone include: Games, School, Camera, Tools, Resources, Shopping, Social Media, Finances, etc. Again, these folders should best meet your lifestyle and the type of applications you frequently use on your smart phones. Once your phone is organized it will feel like a huge relief. Sip up! It will be so easy to access all of your apps right away and you will have no problem finding them.

In regards to phone apps, remember that quality over quantity applies in this case. It's best to have only applications that you use at least once every two months rather than a ton of applications that will just lead your phone into a state of "electronic anarchy."

FAST ACTION IMPLEMENTATION

1. Remove all apps from your phone if you have not used them in the past two months.

2. Create folders for your apps and drag them into each folder. Add these folders to your main home-screen.

Chapter 7:
Music and Creating
Playlists That Work

Stevie Wonder once said, "music is a world within itself, with a language we all understand." In this book we discuss how organization can be therapeutic and is a strategy that can be related to mindfulness. Music works in the same way. Most people find their chosen style of music they prefer, which promotes serenity within themselves and it can assist with calming and relaxing their minds.

However, you'd be surprised to learn that there is a way to make your music and electronic playlists more organized. First thing's first, if you are one of those people that still maintains their CD collection, we need to address how to get rid of these CDs to promote organization. With so much access to efficient and convenient music technology now, we are in a world where thousands of songs can be stored on a single, small device replacing the need for binders and stacks of CDs that take up too much space in the home. Most of us have CDs in a designated storage space and have not even thought to dispose or get rid of them.

Some people seem to hold emotional ties to CDs and find it difficult to part ways with them. However, it's important to be in the right frame of mind and realize what is actually making you hold on to this disc. It should be the actual song that you have an emotional connection or attachment to. Even if we heard the same song from a CD on a smart-device, our emotions and feelings of contentment should still be evoked from that same song no matter the format it is being played on. So once you are able to come to terms with this, you should be able to find a way to either convert your music CDs onto your computers and trash them once you are done with them, or just dispose of them altogether.

I will say however that there are some people who drive cars where only a CD insert is available for music and there is no Bluetooth device in your car that allows you to play music to your phone. If this describes your current situation, there is an easy solution. Almost all cars have an "AUX" insert where you can connect an auxiliary cable (looks like the end of a headphone plug attachment) to your car radio and then connect the end of the cable to the headphone slot in your cell phone or smart device which will allow you to directly play music from your phone to your car radio. Now this bypasses the need for anyone to have CDs at all. There are so many ways to access music that there truly is no use for CDs. The disorganization CDs present in your home outweighs the need to have them at all. So trash them!

Now that we are through with the CDs let's address more deeper organization protocols on how to organize music and playlists on your smart devices. The first thing I want you to do is generate a list of specific times where you often listen to music on your devices. My list would go as follows:

- Commute to and from work
- Working out/gym
- At night/bedtime
- Vacation, by the pool, or by the beach
- Hiking, walking, jogging

Now I want you to create a playlist for each of these categories and make the title of the playlist linked specifically to that setting. Now picture the types of songs or types of music you would want to hear during each of these activities and add songs to your playlist accordingly.

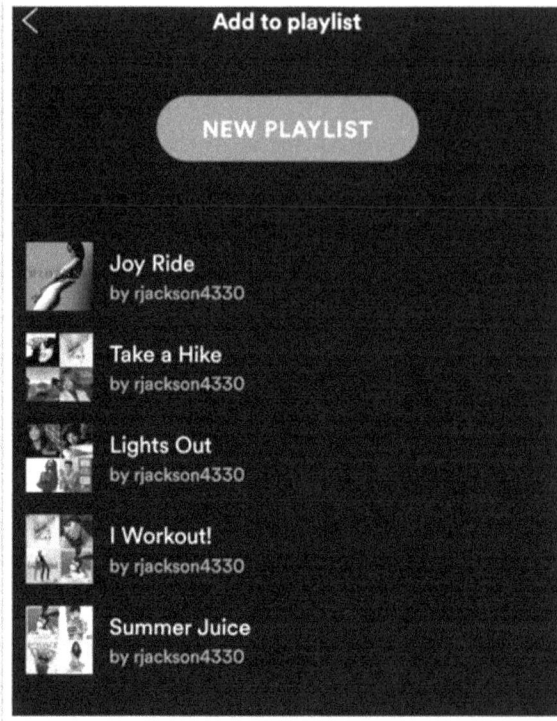

It's important to have playlists with specific, selected songs because we want our moods and goals during these sessions to be enhanced. For instance, you most likely would not be motivated to work-out or "pump some iron" if all of a sudden Whitney Houston's *I Will Always Love You*, suddenly came on while you were at the gym (unless there is an amazing club remix to this song I am unaware of. If so, please contact me and inform me of it). In that same notion, if you were going to bed at night you probably would not be able to fall asleep so easily if a loud and fast rock song started playing.

The music we listen to usually heightens our attitudes and boosts our euphoria. Organization has the same common goal. A combination of the two going hand-in-hand will do wonders for your ease and mindfulness. That glass of shiraz should also do wonders for your ease and mindfulness. You deserve it! Sip up!

FAST ACTION IMPLEMENTATION

1. Make a list of the times or occasions that you listen to music.

2. Develop playlists based on these times and add songs to each one according to your mood during these times.

Chapter 8:
DVDs and DVRs

Now this is a subject I was debating on whether or not to include in this book. However, there are some people that I have come across that do need to develop organizational skills in this department, so I found it necessary to include this section.

Sometimes we find ourselves in situations where we have had such a long work week or we have had an extremely busy weekend and we tend to fall behind on television shows and series that we would normally watch if we were not in such circumstances. The easiest solution to this is to DVR all of your shows you watch and to never actually watch them live or on time unless it's a series finale' that you don't want to run the risk of seeing spoilers on or a show that requires active participation like voting or live tweeting. The reason I say this is because if we were to watch a show's entirety we may be spending a full hour watching it and even sitting through commercials. If you just DVR the show, you have the option to skip the commercials and proceed to the regular program.

Let me give you a mathematical scenario on just how much time you can actually save by utilizing this method. Suppose you have two, hour long shows you plan on watching on a Wednesday night. The first show is at 7:00pm and the second show follows right after that at 8:00pm. If you just decided to watch the shows live, you would spend 2 full hours watching them, from 7:00pm-9:00pm.

However, if you DVR both shows and are able to skip the commercials, you save roughly 15 minutes of commercials per each hour-long show. So now you can actually start the first show on your DVR at 7:30pm and then be caught up to the second show by 9:00pm thereby saving 30 minutes of your time that evening! 30 minutes every day is huge! I'm sure that there are plenty of other productive things you could be doing around your house for 30 minutes on a weeknight or weekend instead of sitting through commercial ads. 30 minutes may seem like not a big deal, but on a weeknight after work where your free time is limited, it is a big deal!

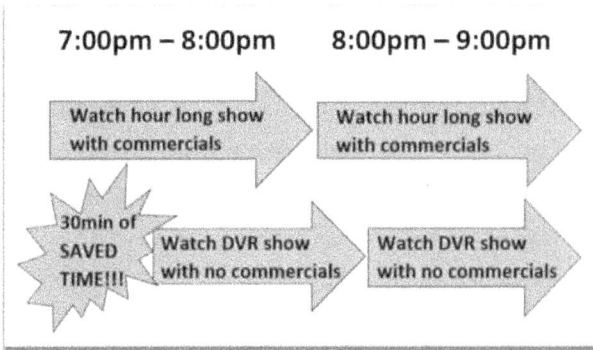

7:00pm – 8:00pm	8:00pm – 9:00pm
Watch hour long show with commercials	Watch hour long show with commercials

30min of SAVED TIME!!!

| Watch DVR show with no commercials | Watch DVR show with no commercials |

As for movies, you would think you would organize your DVDs and Blue-Ray Discs similarly to how I described CDs in the previous chapter. Simply download the DVD to your computer for your own use and keep it on your hard drive. Once it's downloaded you can immediately dispose of it. I would actually caution against this rash decision this time. For one thing, most people prefer watching movies on their big screen televisions. CDs/music can easily be transferred from your computer and right to your smart device, but converting the movies from your computer to a television is much more difficult (and illegal in many cases). Secondly, I recommend keeping your DVDs and Blue-Ray Discs because if you do dispose of them, you would still have to pay roughly $4.00-$6.00 to rent a movie through your cable provider on your television or even buy the movie through your cable provider for sometimes up to $20.00. In order to be more cost-efficient and responsible, keeping your movie DVDs is ultimately the best option for most people.

Now if you do keep your DVDs and Blue-Ray discs, I recommend organizing them so that they take up minimal space and are not invasive in a storage unit. In my lifetime, I have probably accumulated over 600 DVDs and Blue-Ray discs. I am an avid movie watcher and bought so many DVDs between 2005-2015 when DVDs were extremely popular. Instead of disposing of my DVD collection, I decided to remove each DVD from the cover/case and put them in single plastic sleeves. I then bought mini decorative card-board boxes and labeled them like A-C, D-F, G-I, J-L, M-O, P-S, T-V, W-Z. I organized all of my, now protected and sleeved, DVDs alphabetically into their respective cardboard boxes. I then stacked these boxes and placed them in a closet for storage. The amount of boxes you use should depend on the number of DVDs you have.

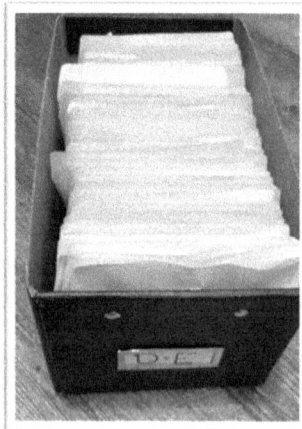

This verifies that all of your movies are in one designated location, they are easy to access based on them being in alphabetical order, and they take up minimal storage space. This is yet another organizational method you can utilize in your own home to give you a sense of relief and happiness. Sip up!

FAST ACTION IMPLEMENTATION

1. DVR or record all television shows/series that you watch. Watch them once they have been recorded so you can fast forward through commercials and save time.

2. Alphabetize your DVD/disc sets and place them in plastic sleeves within a storage container for protection.

Chapter 9:
Photo and Paper Overload

If there has been any type of organizational advice that I have gotten the most praise on from friends and acquaintances who have applied it, it is definitely this one, which is why I saved this as the last piece of electronic organization topic I want to cover. In every home I have been in, people have way too many photographs and papers than they should. I'll start off with how to organize photographs and then we will get into how to handle papers.

In regards to photographs, there is only one simple rule I follow: "IF IT'S NOT DISPLAYED OR ON A WALL, IT DOES NOT BELONG AT ALL!" I want you to repeat this out loud right now to yourself. "If it's not displayed or on a wall, it does not belong at all!" What I mean by this is that if a photograph is not displayed in a frame, on a table, on a shelf, or if it is not hung or shown decoratively on a wall of your home, then you need to get rid of it. Of course, I do not recommend just simply throwing the photographs away. There is a much more convenient way of organizing and storing them so that they are not loose or cluttered around your house and you will have easy access to all of them in one specific location.

For some people this will be a difficult task because of the emotional and sentimental ties most people have. Photographs are extremely powerful to the human mind as they bring up fond memories of the past that promote positive feelings within oneself. So most people find it challenging to part ways with them. I have a solution that will not only allow you to not have to part ways with your photos, but also to better organize them in a way where they take up zero physical space in your home.

So, the first step in the process of organizing your photographs is to collect all of the loose photos in your home that are not displayed in a frame or on the wall. Once you have gathered all of them, you need to categorize them into sections. These sections may be based on the setting within the photograph, the year, the people in the photographs, etc. Now we need to lay all of the photographs in each category out on a clean table or floor in a square or rectangle like below:

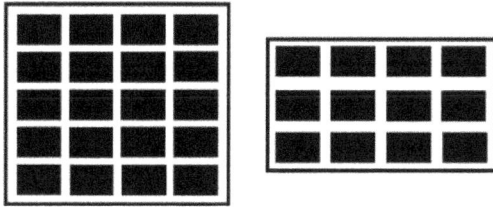

Now that you have one category of photographs laid out in a neat manner, you need to use your phone to download an app that will easily allow you to take a picture, automatically crop the image so that it can be emailed, and sent to your computer or hard drive all into one single file. A recommended application that I frequently use is called "CamScanner" but if worse comes to worse, you can easily just use your normal phone camera and then send the images to yourself.

The "CamScanner" app itself is fairly easy to use and extremely convenient. It even brightens and enhances the photographs for you. No edits or filters needed on your end!

Once you send the photos to a place where you can collect them on your main computer, you can make multiple folders and just drag and drop each photograph into a labeled folder you can easily access at any point in time. You will then want to repeat the process for the other categories/albums of photographs you plan on transferring into an electronic format. Now you can enjoy viewing all of your photos without having to search for specific ones around your house since they are now all in the same location.

I have had many people complete this method of organization in the way I have specified and they have been nothing but grateful for the advice and support I have provided them in helping complete this task. None of them have relapsed into this potential area of "physical anarchy" and are much more pleased with these new, organized results.

The way you organized and converted your photos into an electronic format is almost the same way I want you to organize your papers. I want you to sort and categorize your papers into piles. From there, make folders on your computer where each paper file will go. Lay your papers out on a flat surface and scan each one using the "CamScanner" or a similar application. The app will not only crop your papers, but it will automatically convert them into a PDF file that can be readily transferred to your computer.

Once you are done scanning the papers, you can easily shred or dispose of them. Some people have asked, "well what if I need a hard-copy?" The easy solution is to simply print that file out when you need it, and when you are done with it, shred or trash it once again so you do not relapse into having extra copies of your papers around again.

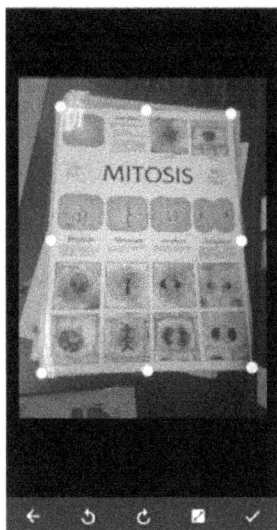

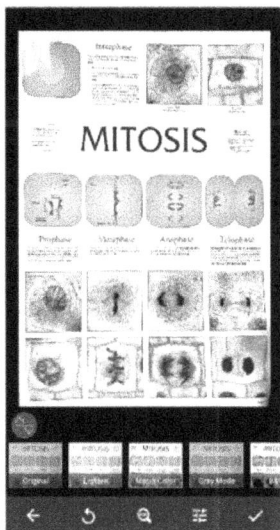

Although you may have to frontload a bit of your time in having to scan all of your photographs and papers into the electronic formats, you will be so pleased with the results, it will all be worth the time and effort put into it. Never again will you have to go through what seems like endless piles of papers, folders, and drawers in your home in search of something that can now be easily found by two or three clicks on your computer mouse.

Everything is restored to peace once again and you can breathe. Close your eyes and enjoy the chill of the chardonnay striking your lips. Sip up!

FAST ACTION IMPLEMENTATION

1. Collect all photographs that are not in frames or on a wall. Transfer them to your computer and then dispose of the hard copies.

2. Collect all loose papers in your home. Transfer them to your computer and then dispose of the hard copies. Only print them out when needed.

PART II – PHYSICAL ORGANIZATION

Chapter 10:
Conquering Your Closets

One thing my friends and family poke fun at me about (though I suspect that they are secretly jealous!) is how organized my walk-in closet is. My closet is one of my sanctuaries in my home! Whether it is a small closet or even a large walk-in closet, I have had experience in handling both of these.

Before you start sorting through clothes, I always use the 75% rule of thumb. Your closet and drawers should never be more than 75% full. I say this because you need quite a bit of room for your clothes to "breathe" and not get wrinkly. Plus, we all know how clothes shopping goes. The rate at which you buy clothes tends to be much higher than the rate at which you get rid of clothes.

I choose not to store my clothes seasonally. They are hung and accessible year-round. I have my hanging clothes organized into six sections:

1. Long sleeve sweater materials

2. Lighter cotton long sleeve shirts

3. Short sleeves and T-shirts

4. Button-down dress shirts

5. Dress pants

6. Suits and blazers

I am a male with a less variety of clothing styles. So, for women, or anyone for that matter, with many types of garments and styles, the sections can go up to 8-10 categories. Once you have categorized your hanging clothes by style, you should then color-code them. Separate them by these main 11 colors: Blacks, Grays, Whites, Purples, Pinks, Reds, Browns, Oranges, Yellows, Greens, Blues. I also like to hang them up in this order too. I find the order of these colors as I have described to be optimal for showing the best transition and contrast through one another. Now once you have your different styles color-coded, you need to sort each color from deeper/darker colors to lighter shades and tones.

Now, let's go over the types of hangers to use. The outer rims of the hanger should be smooth with no divots. The reason I do not recommend divots is because divots wrinkle the shoulders of many shirts and especially heavy sweaters. I prefer my clothes nestled on smooth hangers only. Plastic will suffice. I only use wire hangers for dress clothes like the button-down dress shirts and for suits and blazers which is what dry-cleaners use when you send them out for cleaning. Otherwise, in the infamous words from the movie Mommy Dearest, "NO WIRE HANGERS... EVER!"

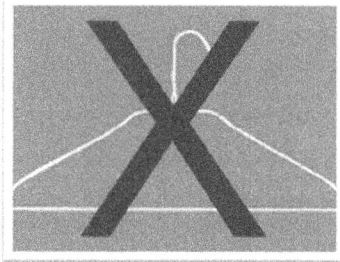

No Wire Hangers

Smooth Plastic Hangers

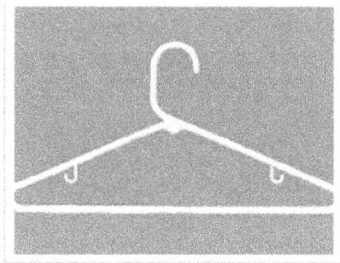

No Hangers with Divots

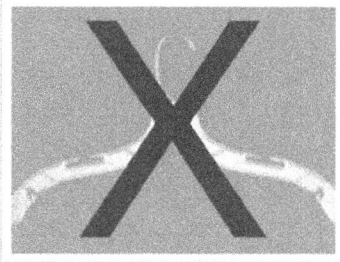

You may find that your closet is way too cluttered and you can't fit all of the recommended shirts on hangers in your closet. This is a sign that you need to declutter some of your clothes. The best way to do this is to take these two factors into consideration when choosing which clothes to get rid of: Have I worn this at least once in the past year? Do I have an extremely sentimental or emotional attachment to this article of clothing (like a bridal gown)? If the answer is "no" to both of these questions, it is a good idea to get rid of it.

When people get rid of clothing from their closets, it should not be a sad experience. People should be empowered and proud by their best fashion choices and pleased with how these clothes had once made them feel. To those clothes that you decide to get rid of and you think are out of fashion and do not do you justice, I want you to toss them to the side and yell "Begone!" Or even if you want to feel more powerful, "Bye, fool!"

Many closets have exposed racks above the poles that their clothes hang from. Up here is where I recommend putting folded jeans, shorts made of thicker materials, and possibly your thickest of sweaters that will never wrinkle when folded, if you have the room. Purses should go up here as well. It's important to also utilize height in the closet. Below your hanging clothes should be a set of drawers where you can fit your socks, underwear and garments. These drawers too should only be about 75% full so that when you open the drawer all contents within that drawer are visible. There should be no socks or underwear that are buried at the bottom of the pile, nor deep in the back. Also, if you have room on the floor next to your drawer, adding a few stacked shoe racks might also be a great use of the space.

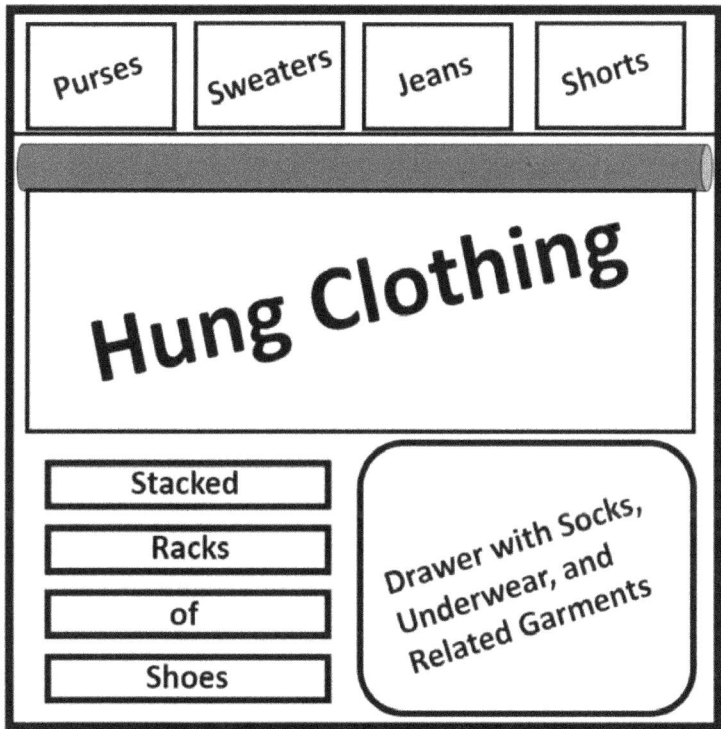

| Purses | Sweaters | Jeans | Shorts |

Hung Clothing

| Stacked |
| Racks |
| of |
| Shoes |

Drawer with Socks, Underwear, and Related Garments

I also prefer to have jewelry and accessories like sunglasses exposed as well. There are plenty of compartmentalized, organized trays that you can easily use for these, that you can typically find at retail stores or from an online retailer.

Allow your clothes to breathe! All clothing should be easily accessible and visible. Treat your clothes as if each and every article of clothing is an expensive designer piece. Most of us know of those few accessories or pieces of clothing that are name brand designers, whether it's a designer purse, dress, pair of shoes, or sunglasses that we have. We all pay careful attention and provide extra care to those specific items that seem to be at the top of the hierarchy of things in our closet. Why not treat all of our clothes just the same and as equally well? Providing quality care to our clothes will lead to a longer quality of life for them.

FAST ACTION IMPLEMENTATION

1. Color-code your hung clothing based on style and then by hues.

2. Place all of your jewelry and accessories into organized trays.

Chapter 11:
Kitchens You Can
Actually Find Stuff In

As an educator, my passion has always been with science, and specifically human biology. I consider the intricacy of the human body to be magical. Every cell, every tissue, every organ, every artery and vein in the body is advantageously placed to make humans the most complex organism on the planet. The human body is nothing but one complete build-up of organization from the smallest of cells to the most complex of organs. Our cells are compartmentalized to get the best functions for the amount of structures present within them. Our organs are shaped, compartmentalized, and organized in just the optimal way to support higher functioning. A kitchen is similar in nature.

The more compartmentalized your kitchen is, the more functional it becomes. Each drawer in your kitchen that holds any sort of utensil including knives, forks, spoons, measuring cups, pizza cutters, ice cream scoops, wine stoppers, bottle openers, can openers, spatulas, etc., should be in a compartmentalized tray. All of these items should be present in all drawers in your kitchen.

Therefore, this allows me to proceed in saying that **ALL KITCHEN DRAWERS SHOULD HAVE TRAYS WITH ORGANIZED COMPARTMENTS**. When you have similar utensils together in a designated drawer and organized accordingly, you get much more use out of them.

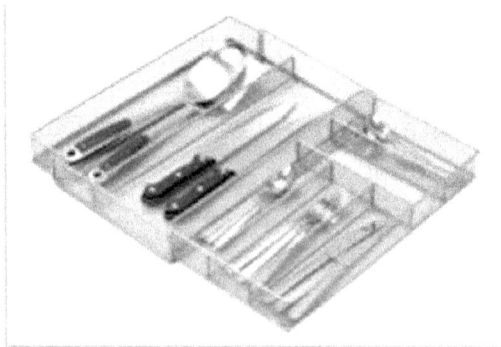

This leads me to my second recommendation when it comes to drawers. Never ever have a "junk drawer" in your kitchen or anywhere in your house for that matter. The fact that the English language has even adopted the term *junk drawer* as an everyday norm and term that almost every person has heard of and knows of goes against the laws of organization. A junk drawer is organization's mortal enemy. So, the moral of this story is to place everything in a designated place where you can find it or if you don't use it, then get rid of it! A junk drawer to me is abysmal and serves no purpose and will never allow anyone to feel peaceful and serene!

In regards to silverware, someone had once asked me how long should they keep their silverware until replacing it. I tell them to look closely at the intricate designs on the handles of most knives, spoons, and forks. When you start to see the slightest trace of rust, it's time to dispose of them. On average, if you take good care of your silverware and do not leave them sitting in a pile of water in your sink overnight repeatedly, your silverware set can last five years or more. I would say I am close to that five year mark, and I can see a slight trace of brown specs on the end of a few of my everyday knives. I will most likely trash them and buy a new set in the near future, myself.

Now that we have covered drawers, let's go over upper cabinets in the kitchen. What goes in your upper cabinets should be kitchenware that will never go into an oven or a stove, and is only meant to go on a table for holding foods or liquids for eating or drinking out of. These items include plates, bowls, cups, glasses, ramekins, glass food trays, and other related items. The one exception to this rule is with spices, herbs, and oils. If you have a small, upper cabinet that you can devote to these materials, that will suffice. If you have an organized structure or rack on your countertop that can hold spices and herbs, that will work as well.

Your lower cabinets in your kitchen should be used for large, bulky items that would typically go into an oven or on a stove like pots, pans, glass baking trays, baking sheets, etc. There are only two exceptions to this rule of lower cabinets. One of them should contain miscellaneous cooking items, like rolling pins, mixers, etc.

Having these items sit in a nice mini basket with fabric in it within an available, lower drawer or cabinet will keep them organized. The lower cabinet that is directly beneath your sink should contain all sorts of cleaning supplies, and trash bags if you do not have a pantry, garage, or main level closet you keep them in. Again, I would have these cleaning supplies in plastic bins. The last thing you would want to happen is for one of these cleaning products to leak and ruin the entire inside of your cabinets. It would be much easier to dispose of the plastic storage container or bin your cleaning products are in, rather than cleaning the entire inner cabinet if by chance a leak were to occur.

My only other major recommendation for the kitchen has to do with items that go on the countertops. Smaller appliances that typically get weekly use should be on countertops, including coffee machines, toaster ovens, and microwaves. These are acceptable to have on the counter's surface. If you find that there is still plenty of bare space on the countertops, then I would recommend adding some decorations. I prefer using tchotchkes (pronunciation: choch-keys) like colored ceramic or glass containers, and grouped into threes, which I will explain why in the "Living Room" section of this book.

Once you re-organize your kitchen into the way I specified, you will feel a warm, melting sensation within your heart, now knowing that behind every closed drawer and cabinet, there is no disorganization or mess of utensils and kitchenware. When you wake up in the morning to make yourself a cup of coffee, you can take your first sip with a pleasant feeling in your body. When you go to bed at night and turn your kitchen light off, you will look back at your kitchen before proceeding upstairs to bed with a smile on your face, knowing the pride you take in your new organization methods you have now applied, to treat your kitchen with respect and dignity. Grab that wine glass and sip up!

FAST ACTION IMPLEMENTATION

1. Make sure compartmentalized/organized trays are in every kitchen drawer full of silverware and related utensils.

2. Remove all items from the "junk drawer(s)" in your kitchen and either dispose of the items or move them to their new, organized designated locations.

Chapter 12:
Bathroom Optimization

Organizing half-baths and guest bathrooms are pretty basic and standard. What I really want to dive into is how to maintain a main or master bathroom in your home. I am praying that you have tile on your bathroom floor, because that makes everything much easier for keeping the area clean and tidy. A carpeted bathroom is just a disaster waiting to happen. Unwanted bacteria lingering in the carpet, a constant need to have to vacuum the bathroom carpet from hair, the carpet getting constantly wet from getting out of the shower, etc., is something we should aim to avoid.

Also, make sure you limit the amount of rugs/mats in your bathroom as well. I would have no more than two or three bathmats or bath rugs in your master bathroom. One should be alongside your tub or shower and the other should be in front of the sink at your vanity. If you have two sinks, then I recommend a small rug for each or a single, elongated rug that stretches the length of both vanity-sink areas.

Just like the silverware in kitchen drawers, bathroom drawers should also have compartmentalized and organized trays to store small bathroom accessories, toiletries, and make-up in. In a separate drawer or storage unit, you may have a larger compartmentalized organizer that contains more elongated items like toothbrushes, toothpaste and lotion tubes, razors, deodorants, etc.

As a personal preference, I like to have a clean sink and vanity. Besides soap or a soap dispenser at each sink, a nice decorative tray to display colognes, perfumes, and other glass materials should be present. It does promote a sort of glamour and elegance to the area, which is the aesthetic goal of a master bathroom. To further add a touch of class to your bathroom, put a bold color of mouthwash in a glass tequila or potion-like bottle on your vanity as well.

In regards to bath towels and washcloths, having at least three sets for rotation is ideal. What I mean by rotation is after you have used a washcloth and bath towel, it should go into a laundry hamper and you should bring in the next set of towels and washcloths for the next use.

When it comes to bath towel storage, I would put the two sets not in use in a linen or bath closet. The washcloths and towels that are ready for immediate use should be hung on a bath towel rod or hook in the bathroom in a neat and orderly fashion.

Utilizing height is an important goal in your bathroom and especially in your shower. Having bottles of shampoo, conditioners, body wash, etc., sitting on the small rims of your shower and bathtub can be a little too brave for being at risk for a spill or fall, and they stand out like an eye sore.

There are plenty of liquid dispensers you can hang from the shower wall and pour the shampoos, conditioners, and body washes into to combat this issue. You should also find hooks that stick to shower walls to hang other items you typically use in the shower, like razors.

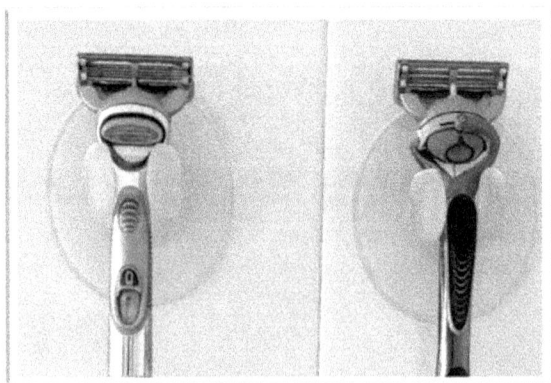

Personally, I have three "sanctuaries" in my house. I mentioned that the walk-in master closet was the first. The second is my master bathroom. I want my master bathroom to look as glamorous as possible. I even installed a mini-chandelier just above my jetted tub, with some candles around it. This creates quite the relaxing ambiance when you dim the chandelier, light the candles, and take a bath with a glass of wine while having smooth jazz music playing.

This organization within my bathroom puts my mind at ease. I am able to take a sip of red wine, listen to Sade's *No Ordinary Love* or a Toni Braxton song and transcend into a mindful state. I hope you can do the same once you have created this warm, relaxing environment in your master bathroom as well. Sip up!

FAST ACTION IMPLEMENTATION

1. Utilize the height in your shower/tub area by having hanging soap dispensers and places to put razors and other items you typically need there.

2. Use compartmentalized and organized trays in your bathroom drawers for loose bathroom toiletries and accessories.

Chapter 13:
Living Rooms You Can Live In

Now here is the place in your home where most people are just itching to get to once you come home from a long, busy day at work. Once you take your shoes off, put away your belongings, and change into more comfortable clothing, you want to just flop down on your sofa and watch television shows to distract your mind from the stress of your work-life or just simply a busy day. The main place you wind up after a long day at work tends to be the living room. Your living room should be spacious and have plenty of floor space to walk across.

The organization of your living room actually lies in how you decorate it. Like my kitchen countertops, I love to add tchotchkes to my living room. I use the same color and style of tchotchkes in a single location but have them at different heights. This promotes elevation to the area where they are located.

As I mentioned in the kitchen section of this book, I group my tchotchkes and decorations into threes. The reason for this is because of its added visual appeal, which thereby makes your mind more pleased and you can enjoy the view of the arranged objects. Take the time to think about it. Since as far back as I can remember, I recall so many home décor magazines mentioning that when it comes to decorations, odd numbers work best. One is too little, and five or more is way too many. Therefore, the magic number is three. Even numbers are symmetrical and do not draw the eye because of the lack of distinction and appeal, when compared to an odd number of similar items. Asymmetry attracts the eye.

Three also is the minimum number our mind needs to recognize any pattern whether the pattern be based on color, size, number, or shape. Two of something does not allow our mind to differentiate and recognize patterns. This "rule of three" increases your visual appetite. Now keep in mind, this can be applied to all decorations in your house and not just your living room. I am only mentioning it here because there are quite a number of decorations in the living room, so it seems to be the most appropriate place to discuss it.

A majority of people I know have more books in their homes than they probably should. These are books they have only read once but cannot seem to part ways with. If you have a shelf in your office or other area of your house that can store your books, that is just fine. However, if these books are scattered in drawers and many other rooms in your home with no purpose, then you should reconsider removing the books you have not read or think you would least likely be willing to read.

There is only one exception to this rule and it is if you utilize your books as what I like to call "colorful coasters" with other decorations resting on them or if the books, themselves, are displayed as decorations. I personally have quite a few books and even catalog magazines in my living room that are ornamental only. Other individuals I have recommended this to, have taken this idea and ran with it, being pleased with the results. Now you can relax on your sofa, prop up your legs, and have a sip of that smooth, red blend.

FAST ACTION IMPLEMENTATION

1. Organize your decorations into groups of three.

2. For any books that are "overflowing" or out of place, use them as "colorful coasters."

Chapter 14:
A Desk You Can Be Proud Of

The office is a bit tricky for someone like me. If my office space, desk, and credenza are not organized to my liking, I am beyond distracted from my work and cannot seem to get this disorganization off of my mind. This stresses me out. Luckily, my metacognition kicks in, and I maintain organization in my office, so this is rarely an issue for me like it once was when I was younger.

Let's start off with the desk. The surface of your desk should only be meant for three things:

1. Computer, keyboard, and/or laptop space

2. Smooth surface for writing

3. Display of decorations or framed photos for yourself and any visitors in the office.

Based on this standard, you should be able to conclude that I recommend there be absolutely no office supplies on your desk. Office supplies should be in a compartmentalized, organized tray, bin, or holder that can go in your desk drawer(s) and cabinet(s) or in your credenza's drawer(s) and cabinet(s).

Of course, there will be plenty of times when you need to pull out paperwork, notebooks, folders, etc., on your office desk in order to be able to work. However, it's imperative to put these belongings away, out of sight, once you have finished working in the office space.

If you choose to leave a few papers or folders out on your office desk with the thought that "I'm going to be coming back here later today to work anyway, so I will put it away then," then you have completely just set yourself up in a trap. This pattern will continue to repeat itself over and over again until your office desk winds up with a massive pile up of papers and folders which now becomes your office "norm." We want to dispose of this "norm" altogether.

Once you enter your clean and organized office, you will be able to take a heavy and prideful sigh of relief knowing that this is an office you can now be proud of and feel at ease to work in.

If you followed my guidelines when it came to paper storage, you should have plenty of storage space in your desk and credenza for nothing but office supplies. Follow these simple rules and your office will look immaculate in no time.

Now for people who work from home or own their own business and don't go into an office away from home, a little more paying attention on their end to maintain organization needs to be done.

When you are in work mode working on client projects or any type of work projects, then of course you will want to have your files, supplies, and everything you need to perform your work in reach. I know several people who work from home and when they take breaks throughout the day, they leave all of their work supplies out. However, before they go to bed at night or when they shut down their office, they tidy everything up then. This is a critical procedure to stick to or it can turn into a messy office if not maintained.

I also know writers who reference books frequently when they are working. If that's the case, then I recommend having your books organized by genre (if you have enough of them) on bookshelves that are accessible. You can still design the bookshelves in a beautiful way that is pleasing to the eye. Here is an example of a well-organized as well as well-designed bookshelf:

FAST ACTION IMPLEMENTATION

1. Remove all objects from your desk except for your computer, keyboard, mouse, and small decorations to avoid clutter.

2. Put office supplies in compartmentalized, organized trays, bins, and holders in your office drawers or credenza.

Chapter 15:
Organize Away,
with a Glass of Cabernet!

Although I have been discussing methods of electronic and physical organization based on traditional rooms and items most people have, there are some areas I cannot address for every single person when it comes to organization. Some people have collections or what some may call "obsessions" that they keep in their home because it gives them joy. These things are okay to have so long as they do not present overflow in your house. I have come across people who have many books, coin collections, old video games, specific figurines, etc. For me, I have what I call a "sanctuary" for my collection of wine, which is my third and final sanctuary in my home.

Wine makes me elated. Whether it's sipping various wines, organizing them, educating people on them, it is still a passion of mine that I care for. So I am glad to be able provide some insight on it.

Not just with wine, but with any of your "unique collections," you should have a designated location for them. My "wine sanctuary" is actually in my kitchen with its own cabinetry and countertops. My wine area cabinets are separated in two sections: cabinets with glasses of wine, and cabinets with plasticware. A major rule in my house is that there should be no glass in my backyard nor by my pool. Therefore, my guests are well aware of this "plastic" cabinet and it contains a wide variety of plastic-ware including plastic wine glasses, plastic cups, and plastic novelties that are meant for the outside and patio.

In my glass cabinet, I have a variety of wine glasses: stemless, stemmed red and white glasses, glasses with graphic labels, champagne glasses, large extravagant glasses with round bulbs and the thinnest of stems (think Olivia Pope from *Scandal*), and even wine glasses in the shape of beakers from a science lab.

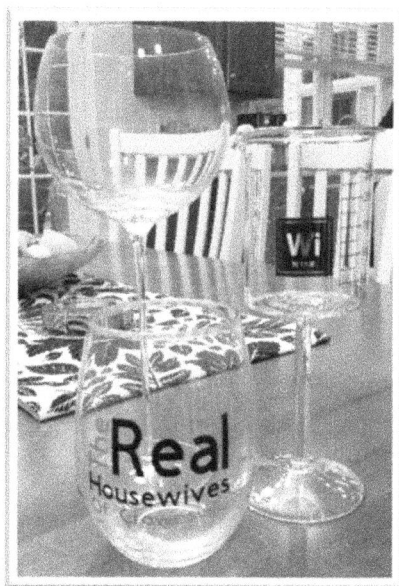

On the countertop, I have a tray of decanters with assorted liquors. A rack on the right side contains white bottles of wine and rosés, while a stacked set of racks on the left contain an assortment of red wines.

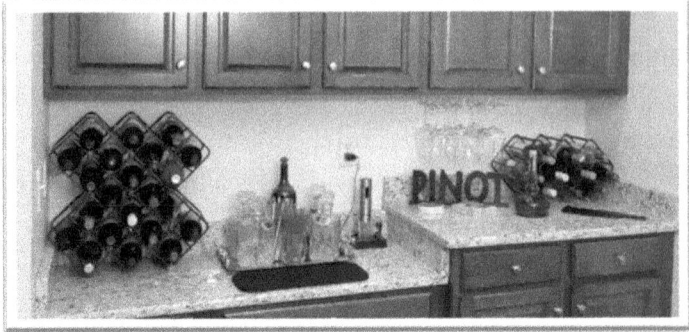

In regards to wine glasses, there is definitely a distinction between glasses meant for whites, reds, and rosés. The more spherical wine glasses are meant for red wines, while the more cylindrical ones are for white wines and rosés. When drinking from a red wine glass you should always hold the glass by the bowl/bulb. The opposite can be said for whites and rosés. When you drink out of white wine glasses you should hold the glass by the stem.

It's easier to remember this rule based on the temperature of the wine. Red wines are at warm and room temperatures, so you can hold the bowl of the glass when drinking them. Rosé and white wines should be chilled, so you want to grip the glass by the stem so as to not have your palm and fingertips exposed to the chilliness of the bowl.

The other rule that I try to abide by is what wine to pair with particular foods. There is a complexity to categorizing each because there are both plenty of red and white wines that go with a variety of foods, but I will try to simplify it for you. Here are the basics:

- Vegetables = dry and fruity white wines, like Pinot Grigio and Sauvignon Blanc
- Dairy Products = sweet white wines, like Moscato and Riesling
- Starchy Foods = rich and oaky wines, like Chardonnay (technically starches can go with most wines though)
- Seafood = almost any white wine, but I prefer sparkling wines, like Champagne and Prosecco
- Light Meats (poultry) = lighter red wines, like Pinot Noir

- Red Meats (beef) = medium red wines, like Merlot and Sangiovese/Toscana
- Cured Meats = dark and bolder red wines, like Malbec, Syrah/Shiraz, and Cabernet Sauvignon.

This may seem a bit complicated so let's simplify even further for when you cannot remember all of these rules: **MEATS GO WITH RED WINES, WHILE SEAFOOD, DAIRY, STARCHES, AND VEGETABLES GO WITH WHITE WINES.**

Of all the chapters in this book I have written thus far, this was by far my favorite, because it is a passion of mine that ultimately makes me happy. You are unique and you should also still take pride in items that make you joyful as there are many ways you can organize them, just like I keep my "wine sanctuary" organized. I thank you for bearing with me as I have rambled on about a passion of mine that may have been a bit of a stretch to relate to organization, but nevertheless there are applicable moments. Needless to say, you should definitely sip up!

FAST ACTION IMPLEMENTATION

1. Make sure you have two sets of wine glasses, designated for red wines and white wines.

2. Separate your drink cabinets by plasticware and glassware.

Chapter 16:
Color-Coding 101

One thing I have not fully discussed is my need for using color-coded organization whenever the opportunity arises. I mentioned a color-coding scheme for clothing, metacognitive and visual learning strategies, planners and schedules, etc. Although I did not go into detail with this, I also utilize color-coding techniques with many of my office supplies and kitchen accessories too.

Research shows that the use of colors increases neural pathways in our brains and the chemical responses at synapses in our brains as well. As a result, our brain is high functioning with the use of colors and color-coding.

I have always believed in the power of color-coding not just for organization, but for better learning and understanding as well, as I mentioned in the meta-cognitive sections of this book. My students are better learners when they have colored visuals and when they organize their notes, binders, and other educational resources into color-codes. I know this to be true, because I have had many of my students complete an experiment to put this theory to the test.

Here is the task I assigned my students:

"You will have 20 seconds to try and remember the specific numbers that are in each shape. Once the 20 seconds are up, try and remember as much as you can and record the numbers from each shape below. You will conduct this memory experiment twice. The first trial will be with shapes without color and the second trial will be with shapes that are colored."

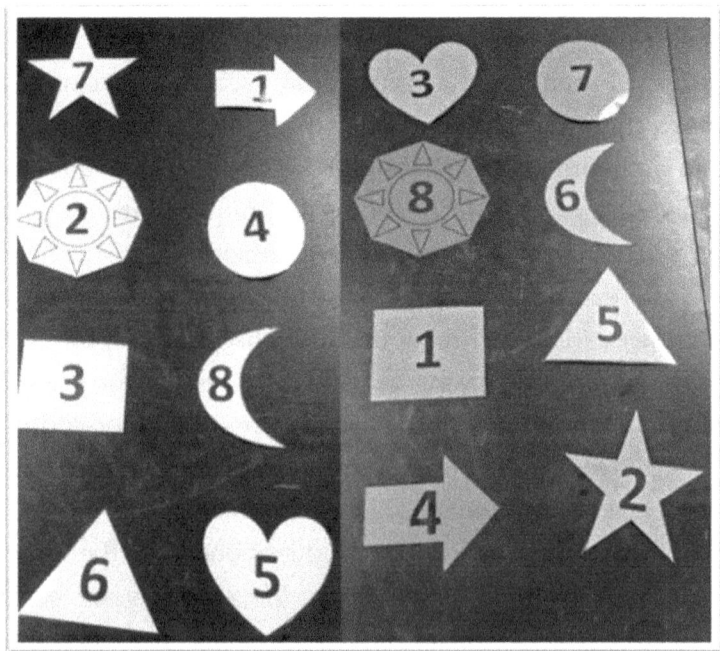

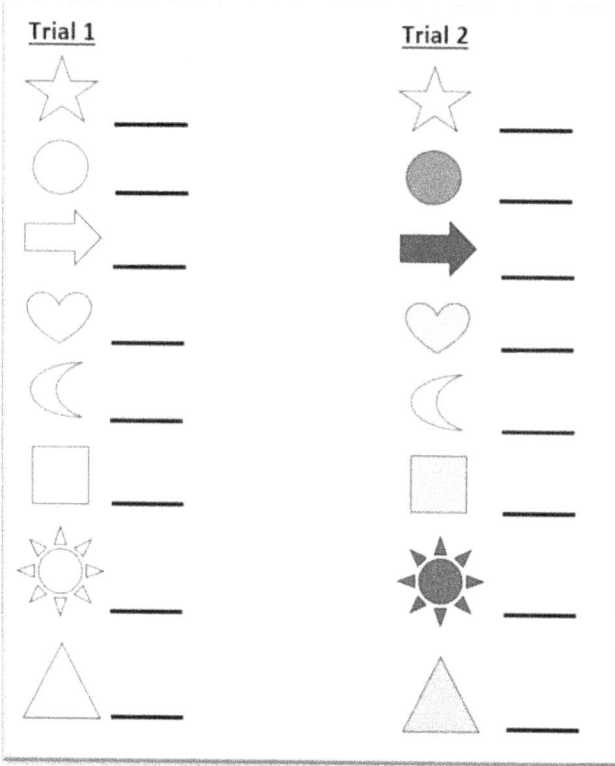

Below were the overall results of the experiment from students I had in class one year. Over the course of four years, all of the results have been congruent. Students were able to memorize the numbers better when the shapes were in various colors. For the group results that are shown, the average score for students when they tried to memorize the numbered shapes without color was 4.08. The average score for students when they tried to remember the numbered shapes with color was 5.05. This is a 12% difference between these averages meaning there is a significance. In previous years, the differences were even greater at 24%, 13%, and 19%, respectively.

Results:

Without Color Trial	
# of Correct Answers	Class Frequency
0	1
1	4
2	19
3	26
4	26
5	24
6	14
7	6
8	5

n=125

With Color Trial	
# of Correct Answers	Class Frequency
0	0
1	8
2	7
3	14
4	19
5	21
6	27
7	8
8	21

n=125

I always have my students reflect on the experiment. I ask them to discuss their ideas and opinions with their groups or partners with answering questions like:

- Was your memory better when using the non-colored shapes or the colored shapes? Why do you think this was the case?
- Based on the overall group data, did more students perform better with the non-colored shapes or the colored shapes? Why do you think these results occurred the way they did?

- How do you think this experiment can relate to school, organization, and memory?
- Did this make you realize anything about your own brain/thinking? Can this help you with organization, memory, or studying in the future? Feel free to mention anything else that comes to mind.

This is one of the many experiments I used to run in the beginning of the school year as a science teacher. This was advantageous to me because not only did it let my students and myself know their preferred learning styles, but it also allowed them to record and graph data, and complete a written reflection which informed me of their experimental, writing, and mathematic skills early on, which would dictate my instructional design for the course of the semester and would allow me to start differentiating, to meet the needs of my students.

I support the use of color-coding, not only because I know that it keeps me organized and supports my learning needs, but that it has helped so many of my former students with their organized and learning styles as well.

BONUS: Organization Chart

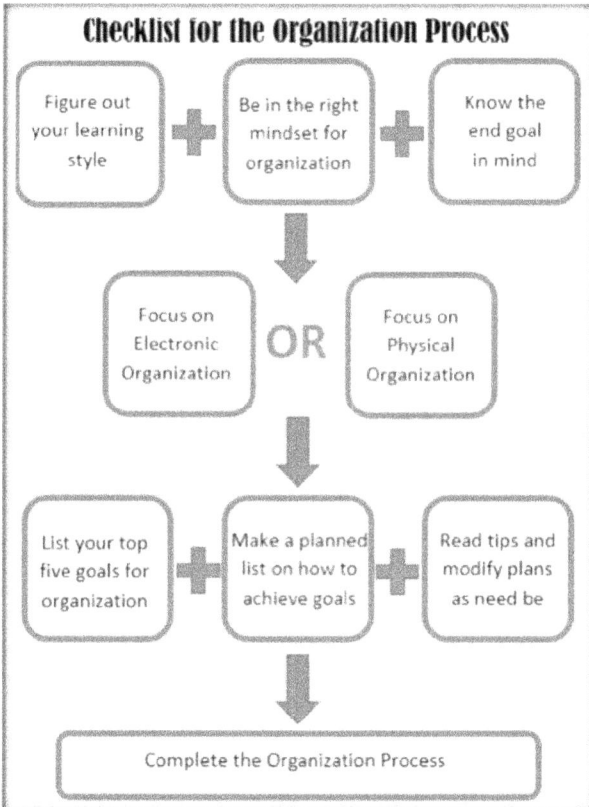

Checklist for the Organization Process

Figure out your learning style **+** Be in the right mindset for organization **+** Know the end goal in mind

↓

Focus on Electronic Organization **OR** Focus on Physical Organization

↓

List your top five goals for organization **+** Make a planned list on how to achieve goals **+** Read tips and modify plans as need be

↓

Complete the Organization Process

About the Author

At age of twenty-nine, Bobby Jackson is already a leader in science education as a Science Teacher Specialist at the Board of Education. He started out as a Biology major in college receiving his Bachelor's degree. From there, he went on to receive two Master's degrees back to back. The first being a Master's degree in Forensic Science and the second being in Secondary STEM Education/Teaching from Stevenson University.

Bobby Jackson has been in the STEM (Science, Technology, Engineering, and Mathematics) education field for over five years.

While in college, Bobby worked full-time as an Ophthalmic Technician for a retina surgeon for over three years while in graduate school. At the same time, he had the opportunity to intern with the United States Secret Service: Forensic Services Division, while receiving his first Master's degree.

Realizing his true passion lied in education, he returned to graduate school to receive his second Master's degree in that area. It was then that his career took off where he became a high school AP Biology and Biomedical Science teacher. He received the 2015 Maryland Association of Science Teacher's New Science Teacher of the Year Award, and then was recognized at the national level as a 2016 National Science Teacher Association's New Teacher of the Year, earning the Maitland P. Simmons Memorial Award for New Teachers.

From there, his leadership roles quickly grew in science education as he became a Science Department Chair, then a Health Science Resource Teacher, to ultimately now being a Science Teacher Specialist, where he provides professional development to kindergarten through twelfth grade science teachers and writing and creating new innovative science curricula and assessments, all the while also working in the collegiate level in STEM education as a graduate professor of STEM Education from his alma mater.

In having such a variety of positions at an early age, all requiring a vast set of skills, Bobby quickly mastered the art of time management and organization skills. He was able to identify these skills prior to college and used them to his advantage. Organization is a skill he values and has promoted in all of his students, teachers, friends, and family. His goal is to expand his audience, by sharing his organizational techniques with the world.

Follow Bobby Jackson on Instagram: @stressy2organized

Summary

If you have implemented any one of my recommended organization strategies then it should be the only time you will ever have to start the process again. Once you have your methodologies and schemes down, the only thing left to do is to just maintain that organization. There should be no need to relapse and end up with a cluttered and disorganized room, computer, phone or living area again.

Remember though, it is imperative that you have self-motivation, a strong-will, and the right mindset before you dive right into the organization process. However, when you do, you will realize just how easy it was to remove all aspects of "physical and electronic anarchy" from your life. Your mind will feel cleansed and you will experience almost a permanent state of invigoration and satisfaction. Organization truly does make me happy and many others that I talk to.

I hope you have found these organization strategies useful and have applied my recommendations. But above all else, I hope organization has brought new beginnings and happy endings to your life… just as it has for mine. Now sip up and continue sipping!